CELEBRATING
HANUKKAH

Library of Congress Cataloging-in-Publication Data
Hoyt-Goldsmith, Diane.
　　Celebrating Hanukkah / Diane Hoyt-Goldsmith; photographs by
Lawrence Migdale. — 1st ed.
　　　　p.　cm.
　　Includes Index.
　　Summary: Presents the history, traditions, and significance of
Hanukkah as it is celebrated by a Jewish family in San Francisco.
　　ISBN 0-8234-1252-0 (hardcover:　alk. paper)
　　1. Hanukkah—Juvenile literature.　[1. Hanukkah.]　I. Migdale,
Lawrence, ill.　II. Title.
　　BM695.H3H69　1996
　　296.4'35—dc20   96-5110
                                                          CIP
                                                          AC
　　　ISBN 0-8234-1411-6 (pbk.)

Acknowledgments
We would like to thank Peretz and Becki Wolf-Prusan and their children, Leora, Avital, and
Noah, for their cooperation and participation in creating this book. We greatly appreciate their
hospitality and enthusiasm. We also are thankful for the participation of other family members
during the holiday festivities: Doris and Hal Wolf, Lilian and Nathan Prusan, Isaac, Bernie, and
Manana Wolf, and Carol, Ron, Elena, Max, and Eva Siegel. We would also like to thank the staff
at Temple Emanu-El in San Francisco for allowing us to include events that occurred at the
synagogue, and the staff of the Jewish Vocational Service. We appreciate the participation of
Reny Wigdor, Katina Price, and the rest of the staff at the Brandeis Hillel Day School. We would
also like to express our appreciation to Pat Schubert, David and Leah Goldsmith, and to Lorna
Mason, for her perspectives as a historian. As always, the comments of our editor, Margery
Cuyler, were most welcome and appreciated.

CELEBRATING
HANUKKAH

by Diane Hoyt-Goldsmith

photographs by Lawrence Migdale

Holiday House – New York

To my school – Noah

To my cat, Zali – Tali

To my friends, teachers, and Israel – Leora

*To our sweet memories of Hanukkahs past
with our grandparents – Becki and Peretz*

The necklace Leora wears was a gift from her mother. It has the Star of David on it. This is also called the Magen David *(MAH-gehn DAH-vid)*, or the Shield of David. It is a symbol of Judaism.

My name is Leora *(lee-OR-ah)*, a Hebrew name that means "my light." I am eleven years old and in the fifth grade. It is winter, a special time of year for my family because we are getting ready to celebrate Hanukkah.

(Top) Leora and her family have many of their own Hanukkah traditions. One of these is preparing homemade pretzels. Leora and her sister, Tali, take pretzel dough and mold it into the shape of Hebrew letters. Their brother, Noah, helps to get the dough ready.

(Left) Leora brushes the top of the dough with a beaten egg before putting the pretzels in the oven to bake.

Hanukkah has been celebrated by Jewish people for more than two thousand years. It is one of my favorite holidays. Hanukkah begins on a different date each year, but it always falls during November or December and lasts for eight days and nights. On the Hebrew calendar, it begins on the twenty-fifth day of Kislev and ends on the second day of Tevet. The holiday celebrates the rededication of the Temple in Jerusalem after its destruction by the Syrians in 168 B.C.E. *Hanukkah* is a Hebrew word that means "dedication."

The Hebrew calendar has been used by people in the Middle East for thousands of years. The calendar we use every day is different. It is called the Gregorian calendar and was named for Pope Gregory XIII, who lived in the sixteenth century. Most of the months — January, February, and so on — are named after Roman gods. The length of each month is determined by the movement of the earth around the sun.

In contrast, the months of the Hebrew calendar are determined by the phases of the moon. This is called a lunar calendar. In a lunar calendar, the appearance of the new moon determines the start of a new month. During Hanukkah, a new moon always appears on the sixth night of the celebration, as the month of Tevet begins.

In about 1300 B.C.E., Moses added the concept of a seven-day week to the Hebrew calendar. Seven is important because each phase of the moon lasts for about seven days. In the Book of Genesis, the Bible tells how God created the world and the heavens during the first six days. On the seventh day, God rested. The Jews called the seventh day the Sabbath. In Hebrew it is called *Shabbat (shah-BAHT).*

Months of the Year by the Hebrew Calendar

Tishri	Sept.–Oct.
Heshvan	Oct.–Nov.
Kislev	Nov.–Dec.
Tevet	Dec.–Jan.
Shevat	Jan.–Feb.
Adar	Feb.–Mar.
Nisan	Mar.–Apr.
Iyar	Apr.–May
Sivan	May–June
Tammuz	June–July
Av	July–Aug.
Elul	Aug.–Sept.

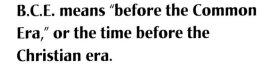

B.C.E. means "before the Common Era," or the time before the Christian era.

7

Leora makes a Hanukkah card for a friend, while her mother and sister, Tali, work on decorations for the house.

The Hanukkah Story

To learn about Hanukkah, we need to go back more than two thousand years. The Jews lived in Judea and Jerusalem was the capital. They worshiped in the Temple, the most important building in the city. Built by Solomon, it had stood for five hundred years as a holy place of worship. In the Temple, the Jews kept the Torah *(TOAR-ah)*, a set of scrolls on which were written the five books of Moses as well as the laws and customs of their faith. The Torah was kept inside a sacred cabinet called an ark or *Aron Ha-kodesh (ah-RON hah-koh-DESH)* in Hebrew. An oil lamp called a menorah *(meh-NOR-ah)* was kept burning in the Temple at all times.

Alexander the Great of Greece and Macedonia marched into Jerusalem in 332 B.C.E. Two years before, his armies had defeated the Persians, gaining control over all the lands that Persia had dominated. Included among these was Judea. The Jews welcomed Alexander and his army into Jerusalem because they knew he was a good leader. After Alexander's death in 323 B.C.E., however, his kingdom was divided between Ptolemy *(TAH-luh-mee)*, the ruler of Egypt, and Seleucus *(seh-LOO-kus)*, the ruler of Syria and Judea.

For the next hundred years, many different kings ruled over Judea. Each ruler was worse than the one before, until Antiochus IV *(an-TEE-eh-kus)* came to power in 175 B.C.E. He called himself Antiochus Epiphanes *(ee-PIH-fah-nees)*, or "the visible god." He thought the Jews should be loyal to him and adopt the Greek language and religion. He wanted them to give up their beliefs and their way of life.

Hanukkah is a good time for stories. Each year, the children hear about the Maccabees and the first Hanukkah. Before going to bed each night, Leora, Tali, and Noah listen to their father read one of their favorite Hanukkah tales.

On his orders, statues of the Greek god, Zeus, were put up in the Temple. Antiochus even stole money from the Temple to finance his wars. Because of these actions, the people of Jerusalem grew to hate him. They called him Antiochus Epimanes (*ee-PIH-mah-nees*), "the madman."

After Antiochus left Judea to lead the Syrian army against the Egyptians, a rumor spread that he had been killed in battle. Immediately the Jews rose up against his followers in Jerusalem. They took down the Greek statues that filled the Temple. They killed the high priest and many others who supported Antiochus.

But Antiochus was still alive. When he returned to Judea, he was filled with rage. His soldiers killed 40,000 Jews as a punishment for their revolt. His Syrian army attacked the Temple and destroyed it. From then on, Jews were forbidden to worship God or to follow their religious laws and customs. This caused many Jews to flee from Jerusalem to live in small villages outside the city. It was in one of these small towns, a place called Modi'in (moh-dee-EEN), that the story of Hanukkah begins.

A Jew named Mattathias (ma-tah-THY-us) lived in Modi'in with his five sons. He was a respected leader, a man of great faith and wisdom. One day, Antiochus's soldiers entered the village and demanded that the Jews kill a pig and offer it to the Greek gods as a sacrifice. According to the laws set down in the Torah, Jews are forbidden to kill and eat pork. Mattathias refused to obey the Syrian soldiers. Another Jew, however, was frightened by the soldiers and came forward to do as they asked. This so angered Mattathias that he grabbed a sword and killed the man. Then he killed the leader of the soldiers. His actions inspired others to fight with him. That day a war between Jews and Syrians began that would last for more than twenty-five years.

Most of the Jews who took up arms to follow Mattathias were poor farmers with only rough farm tools and hand-made weapons to fight with. The Syrians, on the other hand, were well trained and well armed. They rode into battle in chariots, while the Jews fought on foot. As in the Bible story of David who fought the giant Goliath, the Jews relied more upon their faith in God than on their weapons.

Mattathias was an old man when the war against Antiochus began. After he died, his sons led in his place. One son, Judah, was known for his strength. He had the nickname Maccabee, which means "hammer" in Hebrew. Soon all five brothers and the Jews who fought with them came to be called the Maccabees, because they attacked the Syrian army "like hammers."

On the twenty-fifth day of Kislev in the year 165 B.C.E., just three years after Antiochus's army plundered the Temple, the Maccabees won Jerusalem from their enemies. But when they entered the city, they found the Temple in ruins. Immediately they put down their weapons and took up the tools of carpenters and masons. They rebuilt the altar, planted new trees in the courtyard, and restored the ark.

A legend that comes to us tells how the Jews found only a small amount of oil for the Temple lamp. They thought there was enough for only a day or two. Somehow, the lamp continued to burn, lasting for eight days and nights, giving light to the Jews' celebration of joy and thanksgiving. The rededication of the Temple in Jerusalem was an expression of their faith in God and celebrated a return to a Jewish way of life.

When the Maccabees led the Jews against the Syrians, they were fighting against the oppression of a cruel ruler. But they were also fighting for the right to be different. Even though Greek culture had swept into the region on Alexander's heels, they wanted to remain Jews, to worship God, and to live by the law of the Torah.

Today, Hanukkah continues as a celebration of the freedom to worship and to live according to Jewish law and custom.

חנוכה

מן הסם הרדה ניסי נס ... פלשת

Sometimes Leora's father creates pictures out of words. Here the Hebrew characters that spell *Hanukkah* become a menorah.

Hanukkah and Hebrew

Have you ever noticed that *Hanukkah* can be spelled in many different ways? The reason is that it is a Hebrew word. Hebrew is a language with a different alphabet from English. When we write a Hebrew word in English, we try to spell it in a way that sounds like the Hebrew word. However, in Hebrew, there are sounds that don't occur in English. The beginning sound of the word *Hanukkah*, for example, is like an *h*, but starts farther back in the throat. That's why some people spell the name of the holiday with a *Ch* at the beginning, as in Chanukah.

Hebrew is a beautiful language. I am glad that I can study Hebrew in school. We use Hebrew in the synagogue *(SI-neh-gog)*, our place of worship, and in our prayers at home. The Hebrew alphabet of twenty-two letters consists entirely of consonants. Small marks, called vowel points, are added to these to make vowel sounds.

Hebrew is written and read starting at the right and moving to the left. That is why we start at the "back" of the prayer book and read toward the "front." The earliest forms of Hebrew were inscribed on stone. With a chisel in the right hand and a hammer in the left, working from right to left is natural. People writing Hebrew continued that tradition.

Both my father and my mother know how to write in Hebrew. My father is a calligrapher, a person who practices the art of beautiful writing. He tells me that, long ago, calligraphers were called scribes. They were very important because they copied out the Torah by hand.

Leora's father uses a special type of pen to write in Hebrew. He wears a yarmulke *(YAH-muh-kah)* on his head to show respect for God. This cap is also called a *kipah (kee-PAH)* in Hebrew.

Long ago, the scribes made ink from olive oil, pitch, and gum arabic. They wrote on parchment, a strong material made from the skins of animals. The ink did not sink into the parchment the way today's ink does with paper. The first books written in Hebrew were scrolls. Like our Torah scrolls in the synagogue, these early books were rolled up with the right hand from a spool on the left.

During a workshop, Leora's mother goes over the main steps one must take to get a job.

Both of my parents have jobs that benefit people in the Jewish community of San Francisco. My mother works as a counselor in a center that helps people find jobs. The agency where she works is often the first place that Jewish immigrants come to when they arrive in the United States from other countries. My mother helps them get a good start.

My father is a rabbi, a leader of a Jewish congregation. *Rabbi* means "scholar" in Hebrew. In our synagogue, my father is in charge of all the educational programs. He teaches classes for people who want to to learn about Jewish religion, history, and culture.

Many of his students will have a bat mitzvah *(baht MITS-vah)* or bar mitzvah *(bahr MITS-vah)* when they are thirteen. A bat mitzvah is a celebration for girls and a bar mitzvah is for boys. The celebration marks the beginning of a new stage in a Jewish person's life, when he or she becomes responsible for performing *mitzvot (mits-VOT)*. This is a Hebrew word that means "good actions," behaviors that express the values and teachings of the Torah.

To prepare for this special event, my father's students learn how to read Hebrew from the Torah. When my father's students read from the Torah, they are not allowed to touch the parchment surface with their hands. Instead, they use a *yad (YAD)*. Yad means "hand" in Hebrew. It is a silver stick with a hand or finger at one end. Because the Torah is written in Hebrew without punctuation or vowel marks, it is difficult to read it. The yad helps a person keep his or her place while reading and it protects the scroll from oily fingers.

(Top) In the synagogue, Leora's father shows the bar mitzvah and bat mitzvah students the proper way to read the Torah. In the background is a sacred cabinet, called the ark, in which the Torah is kept.

(Left) The students use a special pointing tool called a *yad*.

Celebrating at School

My sister, Tali, and I attend an independent Jewish school called Brandeis Hillel. In addition to our regular classes, we also study Judaism, the religion of the Jewish people. Both Tali and I are learning to speak, read, and write in Hebrew.

We have a lot of fun at school during Hanukkah. Our teachers try to blend the holiday with our daily subjects. We listen to Hanukkah stories, sing songs, and work on holiday art projects. Best of all, during Hanukkah, the school sponsors a night of folk dancing for the students and their families. My friends and I have a good time learning dances that come from Israel.

(Left) **Tali decorates a box with brightly colored shapes of paper. The box will be set up at the entrance to the school to receive student donations for local charities during Hanukkah.**

(Right) **In art class, Leora's teacher helps her finish a Hanukkah menorah made of clay. Later, after the clay has dried, Leora will glaze it. Then she will be able to take it home and use it.**

16

In Tali's classroom, the Hebrew teacher tells a Hanukkah story.
She asks the children to help her act it out.

Celebrating in the Synagogue

During Hanukkah, special events are held in the synagogue. It is a time for Jewish families in the community to celebrate their unity and freedom together.

One special event is for the children who attend the preschool at the synagogue and their parents. During Hanukkah, everyone gathers in a large room to watch as my father lights the candles. The children sit with their parents to hear Hanukkah stories and sing songs.

Leora's father lights the Hanukkah menorah for a special children's service.

My family likes to attend the annual box dinner held at the synagogue. Each family brings a decorated box that holds a picnic dinner. We gather in a large room in the Temple to eat together. Special Hanukkah foods are prepared and delicious Hanukkah cookies too.

During Hanukkah, the young people of the congregation put on a program of songs and readings. Afterwards, we all try the jelly doughnuts called *sufganiyot (SOOF-gan-ee-yoat)*. This special Hanukkah treat is also very popular in Israel.

(Top) Each family decorates a box to bring to the Hanukkah dinner that is held at the synagogue.

(Left) Leora's brother Noah tastes the sufganiyot.

Leora's grandfather holds up her cousin Isaac to see the Hanukkah candles as he is lighting them.

Celebrating at Home

We celebrate Hanukkah at home as well as in the synagogue. Everyone in my family loves the special foods, games, and festive atmosphere that are a part of the holiday.

Hanukkah is also called the Festival of Lights. That is because we light candles just after sundown on each of the eight nights of the celebration. We put the candles into a Hanukkah menorah called a *hanukkiah (han-OOH-kee-yah)*. This is similar to the menorah found in the Temple or synagogue, except that the menorah has places for only seven candles. A hanukkiah has places for nine candles. There is one candle for each of the eight nights of the celebration, plus one extra. The ninth candle is called the *shammash (SHAY-mehsh)*, which means "servant" in Hebrew. This is the "helper" candle, the one we use to light all the others.

First we light the shammash. Then we use it to kindle the other candles. According to Jewish tradition, a day begins at sundown and lasts until sundown the next day. So we begin lighting the candles at sundown on the day before the holiday begins. We let the candles burn each night until they go out completely.

We start by lighting one candle on the first night, two on the second, and so on until all the candles are lit on the last night. When we light our hanukkiah, we put in the candles beginning on the right, then light the candles from the left. That way, the newest candle is lit first each night. We use forty-four candles for each hanukkiah during the Hanukkah celebration.

Leora uses the shammash to light the candles in the hanukkiah.

Each time my family gathers to kindle the Hanukkah lights, we say blessings, or prayers. The first two prayers are said every night, but a special prayer is included on the first night as well. This prayer thanks God for keeping us safe and bringing us together to celebrate Hanukkah again.

After lighting the candles, we sing or chant the prayers in unison. Usually we say the prayers in Hebrew, but when we have guests or visitors, we also say the prayers in English so that everyone can participate.

A Blessing for the Candles

Blessed art thou, Lord, our God, Ruler of the Universe, who has sanctified us by your commandments and commanded us to light the Hanukkah lights.

HEBREW

Baruch atah Adonai, Eloheinu melech ha-olam, asher kideshanu b'mitzvotav vitzivanu l'hadlik ner shel Chanukah.

Giving Thanks for Miracles

Blessed art thou, Lord, our God, Ruler of the Universe, who has performed miracles for our ancestors in times of old, at this time of year.

HEBREW

Baruch atah Adonai, Eloheinu melech ha-olam, she-asah nissim lavotanu ba-yamim hahem bazman hazeh.

Prayer for the First Night

Thanks be to you, Lord, our God, Ruler of the Universe, for keeping us alive and in good health and for bringing us together.

HEBREW

Baruch atah Adonai, Eloheinu melech ha-olam, shehechiyanu ve-kiymanu vehigianu lazhaman hazeh.

The children walk in the park with their grandparents who are visiting during Hanukkah.

Leora's father prepares the latkes for the Hanukkah party.

Hanukkah is a special time because we get to see our grandparents, aunts, uncles, and cousins. When they visit, we go for walks together, play games, and catch up with each other.

One of the best parts about Hanukkah is having a latke (*LAT-keh*) party. Latkes are hot potato pancakes and an important Hanukkah tradition. Latkes are made by mixing grated potatoes, onion, and eggs together. Then this mixture is fried in oil until the latkes are golden brown and crunchy. We eat them with sour cream and homemade applesauce.

The tradition of eating latkes on Hanukkah comes from Jews who lived in Eastern Europe. Latke is a Yiddish word for "pancake." The oil in which they are fried reminds us of the first Hanukkah and the legend of the oil that burned in the Temple lamp for eight days and nights.

Leora's Family Recipe for Latkes

(Adult supervision is necessary for this recipe.)

3 large potatoes, grated
1 small onion, grated
2 eggs, beaten
2 tablespoons flour
1 teaspoon salt
pinch of pepper
vegetable oil for frying

To make latkes, mix the grated potatoes and onions with the eggs, flour, and seasonings. Then heat the oil in a large frying pan. Add the pancake batter to the oil in large spoonfuls and fry until golden brown. Turn the pancakes and fry the other side. Serve the pancakes hot with applesauce and sour cream.

The best part of a latke party comes when everyone is sitting down and the pretty Hanukkah candles are glittering on the mantel over the fireplace. There is delicious food on the table and everyone is eating and talking. Then we know that Hanukkah is here.

Leora and her family enjoy the latkes and being together.

What the Hebrew Symbols Mean in the Dreidel Game

 nun: ב
The player does nothing. The next person spins.

 gimel: ג
The player takes everything in the middle. Each player must put in another marker before the next person spins.

  heh: ה
The player takes half the markers in the middle, or half plus one if there is an uneven amount.

 shin: ש
The player must put one of his markers in the middle.

Dreidel - A Hanukkah Game

Dreidel (*DREY-dul*) is a fun game to play during Hanukkah. I enjoy teaching it to my friends. To play, you need a kind of spinning top called a dreidel. It is often made of wood, but it can also be made of metal, silver, ivory, ceramic, or plastic.

There are four Hebrew characters on the sides of the dreidel. They are *nun, gimel, heh,* and *shin*. These four Hebrew characters are the first letters in a four-word sentence that means "A great miracle happened there."

Children have been playing dreidel for hundreds of years. Some people say that the tradition comes from the days when Antiochus IV forbade the Jews to worship. Young boys who knew phrases of the Torah by heart met secretly to discuss the holy books. If Syrian soldiers saw them together, the boys would start to throw a little wooden top. That way the soldiers would think they were just playing – not studying and praying as they were forbidden to do.

The game we play today comes from the Middle Ages, and the rules are borrowed from a German gambling game that is played with a four-sided top.

How to Play Dreidel

You need two or more people to play dreidel. Each player begins with the same number of markers. The markers can be buttons, pieces of popcorn, coins, or Hanukkah gelt – which are pieces of chocolate shaped like coins. The players take turns, from left to right, spinning the dreidel. The game begins when each person puts five markers in the middle.

One person spins the dreidel. When the dreidel stops spinning, it falls over. The Hebrew letter that is on top will tell the player what to do. For example, if the Hebrew character *nun* is on top, the player does nothing. However, if *gimel* is on top, the player takes all the markers in the middle. With each Hebrew character, there are different instructions. The game is over when one player has won all the markers.

Leora enjoys teaching others about Hanukkah traditions. She and her friend, Leah, play the dreidel game to see who can win the most Hanukkah gelt.

Shabbat Shalom on Hanukkah

Each year, one night — and sometimes two nights — of Hanukkah falls on our weekly celebration of the Sabbath. Shabbat, as we call it, begins at sundown each Friday evening with a candle-lighting ceremony and prayers. Then we have a special family meal. On this night, we light the hanukkiah for Hanukkah first, then we light the candles for Shabbat. We like to invite other people to share Shabbat with us. Our meal on Shabbat combines all the good spirits of Hanukkah with the religious ceremony that we have each week in our home.

(Left) **Leora's brother Noah made this hanukkiah out of nuts and bolts. Tiny candles for a birthday cake are a perfect fit.**

(Top) **Leora and her mother prepare snacks to serve their guests for the Hanukkah meal on Shabbat.**

26

On Shabbat during Hanukkah, the Hanukkah candles are lit before the Shabbat candles. This is because Shabbat marks the day of rest, and there can be no kindling of fires after it has begun. Leora and her family sing a Hanukkah song as they watch the candles burn.

In Leora's family, each child has a hanukkiah and lights the candles each night during the holiday.

Hanukkah Gelt and Other Gifts

The giving of gifts on Hanukkah is also a part of our tradition. Long ago, coins were given as presents to children during the holidays. This came about because, after the defeat of the Syrian army, the Jews were independent for the first time in many years. They were free to mint, or make, their own coins. Gladly they threw away the coins that pictured Antiochus IV. They replaced these with coins that showed the likeness of their new leader, Judah Maccabee.

Gelt is a Yiddish term for "money." Some people still like to give money as gifts on Hanukkah. My parents usually give us Hanukkah gelt in the form of chocolate shaped like coins.

We exchange some gifts on Hanukkah, but our parents try hard not to make them the major focus. Sometimes my parents come up with a theme for the season's gift giving. One year, we all bought or made things that would keep us warm. We got hats, gloves, sweaters, and mufflers. Another year, all the gifts had to be handmade. I think having a theme makes the gift giving fun.

During Hanukkah, we try to think about all the gifts we have received during the year from our family, from the school and synagogue, and from our community. It is important, at this time of year when we are counting our blessings, to give something back in return.

In our home, we have a *tzedakah (tsah-DAH-kah)* box on the table. Tzedakah means "justice." We think it is "right" for people to have food, clothing, and shelter. Giving to others is one of the joys of Hanukkah.

Noah and his cousin, Isaac, put a few coins into the tzedakah box that is always on the dining room table. At a time when the family is celebrating its own blessings, the children also think of those who are less fortunate.

(Top) Leora's brother, Noah, opens a Hanukkah gift. He is happy to get a ball to play with.

(Right) Leora and Tali take the coins from the tzedakah box and use them to buy canned food. They donate their purchases to the local food bank.

Hanukkah has ended, but Leora and her family are still filled with good feelings as they share a sunny winter afternoon together at the beach.

Hanukkah celebrates an event that happened thousands of years ago. The rededication of the Temple in Jerusalem might have been forgotten, but by lighting Hanukkah candles each year, we remember the story of the Maccabees. Their faith and their struggle for freedom inspire us today.

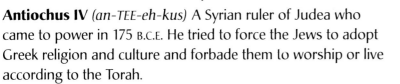

GLOSSARY

Antiochus IV (an-TEE-eh-kus) A Syrian ruler of Judea who came to power in 175 B.C.E. He tried to force the Jews to adopt Greek religion and culture and forbade them to worship or live according to the Torah.

bar mitzvah (bahr MITS-vah) A ceremony held when a Jewish boy is thirteen years old to celebrate his coming of age to religious responsibility.

bat mitzvah (baht MITS-vah) A ceremony held when a Jewish girl is thirteen years old to celebrate her coming of age to religious responsibility.

B.C.E. An abbreviation for Before the Common Era. This corresponds to the time before the Christian era.

C.E. An abbreviation for Common Era. The Common Era is considered to be the time since the beginning of the Christian era.

dreidel (DREY-duhl) A four-sided spinning top with a Hebrew character on each side. It is used in a game, also called dreidel, that is played during Hanukkah.

gelt The Yiddish word for "money," often given as a gift during Hanukkah, either as real money or as chocolate candy shaped like coins.

hanukkiah (han-OOH-kee-yah) A candelabra for Hanukkah with places for eight candles and one shammash.

Hebrew The ancient language of the Jewish people in which the Torah and the Old Testament of the Bible were written. Hebrew is still spoken in Israel and used in Jewish religious ceremonies all over the world.

Judaism The religion of the Jewish people based on the teachings of Moses and the writings of the Old Testament and the Torah, and the culture and way of life based on this religion.

latke (LAT-keh) The Yiddish name for a potato pancake, a dish served during Hanukkah that symbolizes the oil that burned for eight days and nights in the Temple.

Maccabee (MA-cah-bee) A Hebrew word that means "hammer" and the general name for the Jews who followed Mattathias and his sons to fight against the Syrians.

Mattathias (ma-tah-THY-us) A religious leader and an elder who, with his five sons, started the war of independence against the Syrians and led them to victory.

menorah (meh-NOR-ah) An oil lamp used in the ancient Temple in Jerusalem and still found today in synagogues all over the world in the form of a candelabra with seven branches.

rabbi The leader of a Jewish congregation in a synagogue, or a teacher of Judaism.

Sabbath A day of rest and a time to worship God. In Jewish households, the Sabbath begins at sundown on Friday and ends just after sundown on Saturday.

Shabbat (shah-BAHT) The Hebrew word for the Sabbath.

shammash (SHAY-mehsh) The "servant" or "helper" candle used to light the other candles during Hanukkah.

sufganiyot (SOOF-gah-nee-yoat) Hot jelly-filled doughnuts popular during Hanukkah, especially in Israel. This treat, cooked in oil, is a tradition that comes from the Hanukkah celebrations of Jews from the Middle East and North Africa.

synagogue A place where Jews gather to worship.

Temple The center of Jewish life and religion, first built by Solomon in the ancient city of Jerusalem. The Temple was destroyed and rebuilt twice at the same location.

Torah (TOAR-ah) Sacred parchment scrolls on which are recorded the five books of Moses, as well as Jewish laws and customs.

tzedakah (tsah-DAH-kah) A Hebrew word that means "justice." A tzedakah box is used to collect coins that will be donated to charity.

yad (YAD) A silver tool with a hand or a finger on one end that is used as a pointer by those reading the parchment scrolls of the Torah.

Yiddish A language developed out of German that contains a number of Hebrew words and is written in Hebrew. Yiddish is spoken by the Jews of central and eastern Europe and their descendants.

The Eight Nights of Hanukkah

Do Something Special
on Each Night of Hanukkah—

*Some Ideas from Temple Emanu-El
in San Francisco, California*

First Night – Celebrate Freedom
Make a list of freedoms and privileges.
Make a list of people who do not have these
freedoms and privileges.

Second Night – Celebrate Family
Have a latke party.
Invite a friend who has never celebrated
Hanukkah.

Third Night – Celebrate Knowledge
Read the Torah.
Buy a book at the book fair.
Read a new book.

Fourth Night – Celebrate Hope
Help a friend.

Fifth Night – Celebrate Generosity
Take money from your tzedakah box
and buy food to contribute to a food drive.
Volunteer to do something for someone else.

Sixth Night – Celebrate Peace
Make up with someone
with whom you have had a fight.
Make a list of well-known peacemakers.

Seventh Night – Celebrate Equality
Share a toy, game, or possession.
Find something that you do not need
anymore and give it away.

Eighth Night – Celebrate Faith
Write your own prayer for freedom.
Find a poem, story, or prayer that celebrates
freedom and read it to your family.

INDEX

(numbers in italics refer to pages with photos)